C000075729

Shark

FEAR AND BEAUTY

JEAN-MARIE GHISLAIN

Shark

FEAR AND BEAUTY

Thames & Hudson

On the cover: (front) Grey reef sharks, French Polynesia
(back) Osprey Reef, Australia

Translated from the French by Paula Cook.

Design by T'ink Studio, Brussels
Lithography (8 colours) by Mathildestudios, Grembergen (B)
Printed and bound by New Goff - Graphius Group, Ghent
on paper Symbol Tatami 150 gsm.
with the support of Fedrigoni, Verona

First published in the United Kingdom in 2014 by Thames & Hudson Ltd,
181A High Holborn, London WC1V 7QX

Original edition © 2014, Marot S.A., Brussels and the author
Photography and text © Jean-Marie Ghislain / No Headache
This edition © 2014, Thames & Hudson Ltd., London

British Library Cataloguing-in-Publication Data
A catalogue record for this book is available from the British Library

ISBN 978-0-500-51773-4

Printed and bound in Belgium

To find out about all our publications, please visit **www.thamesandhudson.com**.
There you can subscribe to our e-newsletter, browse or download our current
catalogue, and buy any titles that are in print.

CAN BEAUTY CURE FEAR?

Initiation

I am neither a scientist, nor an artist, still less a writer. I am a photographer, and all I did was jump into the water, overcome my fear and come back with some evidence: a few hundred photographs. My only intention here is to share the emotions I felt during my encounters with sharks. Through these images I have tried to convey as directly as possible the beauty and violence that is ever-present in the undersea environment and in the mind of its inhabitants.

The aim of these words is to set the stage for an adventure that took me far beyond my wildest expectations. I embarked on this journey as an initiate, without really imagining how my life would be changed. On each trip, I devoted every ounce of my energy to shooting the best possible images. As soon as I was out of the water, I would begin a provisional edit of the best images straight away, and then – obsessively, all through the night if need be – I would go over every moment of the shoot in my head, analysing every one of the day's shots in minute detail. Ultimately, there would be just one question on my mind: how could I do better in the same circumstances? This obsessive approach meant that I could not rest until I had completed my task, and that left little room for a travelling companion. For a long time I considered this to be a personal failure, but today I know that in fact it allowed me to complete the project.

we are part of a whole, and to perceive the ties that bind us to creatures that are so different from us. These ties are fragile, indefinable, yet we can begin to perceive them by swimming with them. Sharks are capable of teaching us vital lessons. In the cruel world of the sea, there is no room for pride; only survival counts. If you have to lose a power struggle, then so be it – you just have to leave the arena. If you are not totally focused on the immediate task at hand, or if you are not completely relaxed when you enter the water, then these encounters can become very dangerous.

The quest for beauty

I speak of beauty without pretension. The quest for beauty is part of my life, just as one may seek a sense of good or justice. We are not all born equal before beauty. It is too often a luxury that few of us can afford. Beauty is the subject of an existential preoccupation that I owe to my mother, but also to the significant influence of a philosophical context. With humility, I have tried to call upon this sense of beauty in these images of the last truly wild universe, of the marine landscape and its inhabitants.

Obviously, every circumstance that drives you to seek out what lies behind your fears is personal. Yet we are all obliged to face up to our limitations at some point, before we can contemplate extending our horizons. For myself, I realize now just how slowly but surely the whole process has come to maturity and how I have had to experience a chain of events and meetings before I could reach a point at which I could recognize this decision and, more importantly, act upon it.

Changing perceptions

The purpose of this quest was to come into contact with sharks and to find another way of looking at them. In other words: to try to change our perception of these creatures. Ever since my very first dive with sharks in Mexico, I have been touched by their beauty and power. Above all I was made aware of their vulnerability – they need help if they are to avoid rapidly disappearing altogether. Above all, I also experienced an intensity of sheer joy that I had never felt before. This became an unconscious part of my approach.

Did I need courage? I don't think so. You can dive up to certain limits without risking your personal safety. But a solo journey imposes tough demands: you have to have the capacity to live your own life without crutches. My solitude taught me how to live, to understand how much

Rhythms of life and death

What have I sought in deep oceans that I did not find in my many therapies, shamanic sessions and personal philosophical journeys? Being reborn, finding peace, harmony, happiness, truth, a part of my own animal nature, and God knows what else. Why was I drawn to sharks? It probably wasn't necessary. Yes, I could have swum with dolphins, or whales… but I probably needed a powerful electric shock for the emotional patterns to dissolve, leaving room for a major personal evolution, revolution even. The ever-present potential threat of the sharks fed the morbid component of the quest: confronting death in order to realize that you want to live.

It took me three years to understand that behind this quest lay a much more complex motivation, without which I would have found neither the strength nor the willpower to overcome all the obstacles in my way. To begin with, my friends and family tried to talk me out of entering a world that was not my own: 'You don't know the first thing about diving, or about underwater photography'; 'You're afraid of the water'; 'It's dangerous'; 'Think of your daughter'; 'Think of your age', etc. They were all reasonable things to say, but what was driving me on this adventure was not 'reason' but the rhythms of life and death.

Knowledge, love and respect

Why describe these personal motivations in the preface to a book? Probably because this book is also about fear and beauty, life and death. This very personal spotlight is all about understanding that I don't lay claim to these motives on anyone else's behalf – just mine.

Encountering wild animals in general, and predators in particular, brings on feelings of fear. It is above all else a collective fear, transmitted through the generations, which today has become ever more rare as in our western world we are confronted less and less by risk or danger. But the mere thought of this possibility of danger is enough to trigger an uncontrollable visceral fear.

Deeply inscribed in our cellular memory, fear returns when we near the limits of the known world and enter a potentially hazardous universe. To dispel fear requires a constant effort: we must confront what triggers it and replace it progressively with sensations of knowledge and comfort. This is a necessary level of awareness, and we must never allow ourselves to lose sight of the need to stay watchful and respectful of basic safety rules.

Speaking about sharks is as infinite as speaking about people. One meets different characters everywhere, and therefore a very diverse set of relationships exist. On the same day, I came across two great white sharks that were so different from one another that I could have told you everything about them, and the opposite too, with the utmost objectivity. One, an aggressively territorial young male, harassed and jostled me physically to the point of forcing me back into the cage. The other, a female more than 5 metres long, 'played' with me for more than an hour and followed me to the surface, letting me stroke her. So let's cast generalities aside.

What touches me most about these encounters with sharks is the evident richness of their character and the intelligence they show in their capacity to integrate a new element and adapt their behaviour accordingly. Aware of my own utopian approach, I have always tried to put myself in their skin in order to try to understand their reactions. I have been able to experience encounters with them that would be unimaginable with dolphins or whales, witnessing great gentleness and mutual respect, far from the usual clichés. The photographs speak for themselves.

Among the initiated, the debates continue about what is permissible in photography in general and in underwater photography in particular. As far as I'm concerned, having spent a long time investigating the subject, I decided to stick wherever possible to natural light and to work with a focal length as close to that of the human eye as feasible. Purists will no doubt criticize me for 'cleaning' my images as I edit and/ or reframe them. A shoot can only ever be an interpretation of reality. Most underwater photographers I know work with 10 to 15 mm focal lengths and almost all of them use a flash. Isn't that also an interpretation of reality? The medium in which we are evolving has many constraints. Generating high-quality images without using artificial lighting does limit the result considerably, which is why I have chosen black and white when the saturation of blues reaches its maximum point. On the other hand, images shot in natural light allow the atmosphere on the day in a particular location to be very faithfully rendered.

In some cases, there are white particles present in the water, or other fish swimming close to the subject and breaking the composition of the frame, that can substantially influence the general impression conveyed by the photograph, and the desired emotional impact can be affected. I decided to privilege this general impression and so I have intervened just occasionally to make the image simpler for the viewer to take in. These interventions are rare, yet the situations themselves are still rendered as they were experienced and no new element has been added.

All of these images required adjustments of contrast, clarity, exposure, intensity and the correction of dark and bright tones. This work is essential when starting off from a raw file if you want to obtain the best possible result.

Sharing Nature

I experienced such truth and simplicity during these encounters! Now I can observe just how deeply my very being has been transformed, and the extent to which my relations with others have changed. I have become more demanding towards others and towards myself, more sincere in my human relationships, more joyful, tender and compassionate. I have been made more conscious of the urgency to define a new relationship with nature in general and with individual species, to recognize their specific intelligence, their legitimacy, and to give them back their space without systematically trying to impose our superiority.

Many marine spaces are literally empty… Once sharks have been eliminated we may witness a collapse in the food chain that will create a marine desert within a few years. No species can be protected without considering the food chain as a whole. As soon as we understand that, we can no longer stand idly by. We urgently have to manage the oceans in a dynamic way by means of concrete actions. I sincerely hope that this book will encourage and stimulate a new way of looking at sharks, and that readers will want to engage with protecting sharks. The trials faced by sharks are unacceptable, even if the fear underlying them is understandable. It is easier to blame this hated and feared creature than to seek to understand the complex causes and circumstances that have contributed to incidents for which sharks themselves are so rarely to blame.

Dangerous animals elsewhere on the planet have already been eliminated in order to make our lives feel safer and more comfortable. There are virtually no dangerous beasts left in our countries, to the point where some people are attempting – with varying degrees of success – to reintroduce them. Will we really reach that limit with our oceans too, even if the consequences will be far more dramatic for balance of life on our planet?

During my travels, I was lucky to meet more than thirty species of sharks as well as various other marine species, including seals, dolphins, whales, sperm whales, and tortoises. I was accompanied at different stages by two freedivers, South African Hanli Prinsloo and, more recently, Leina Sato from Japan.

I would like to thank everyone who allowed me to go on this journey of initiation: Pablo, Yves, Hanli, Martin, Steve, Mike, Leina, who, like so many ferrymen, have let me pass through the successive stages of my voyage. A special thank you to my daughter Marie-Charlotte for her patience and understanding. There were long months when I was absent, during which she worried about my wellbeing, and had to face a modern life filled with uncertainties on her own. May your life be as rich as mine has become since I have seen what was hidden behind my fears. I feel closer to you than ever before and there is no gift more wonderful.

J.M.G.

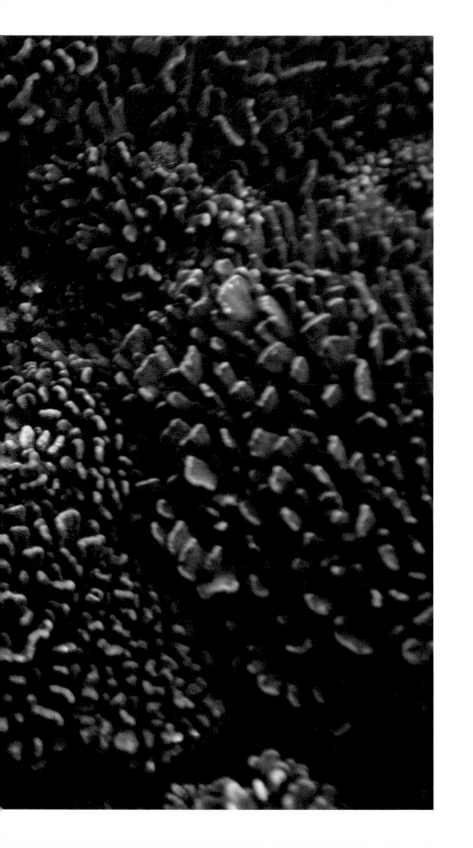

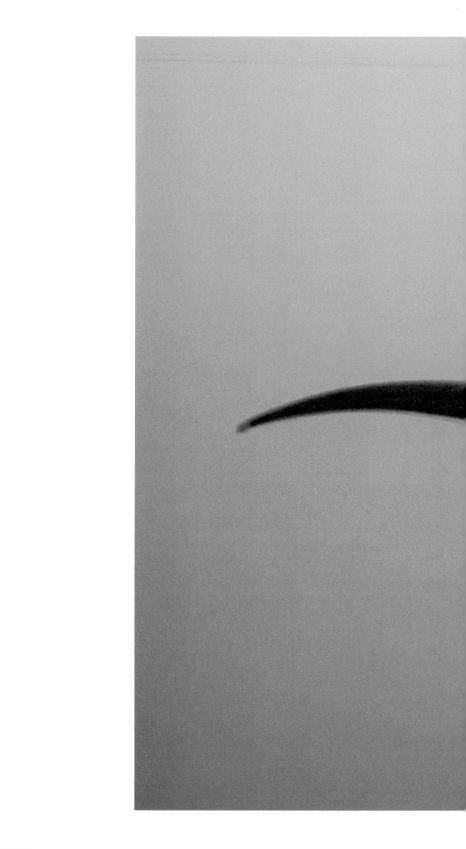

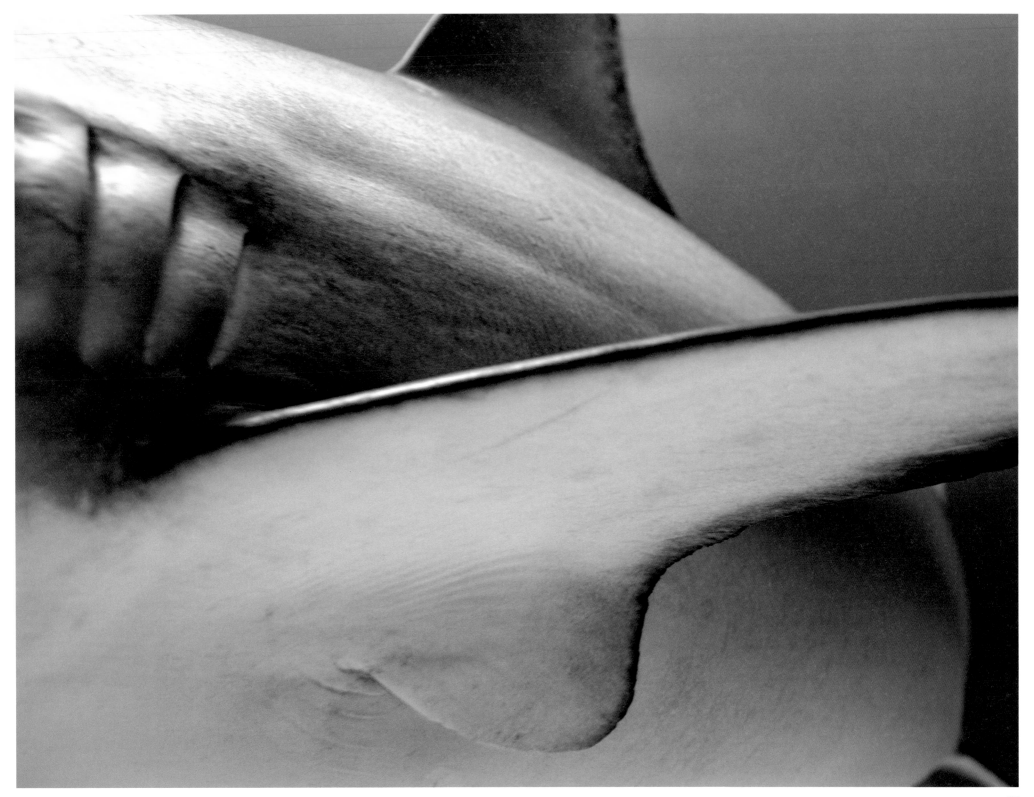

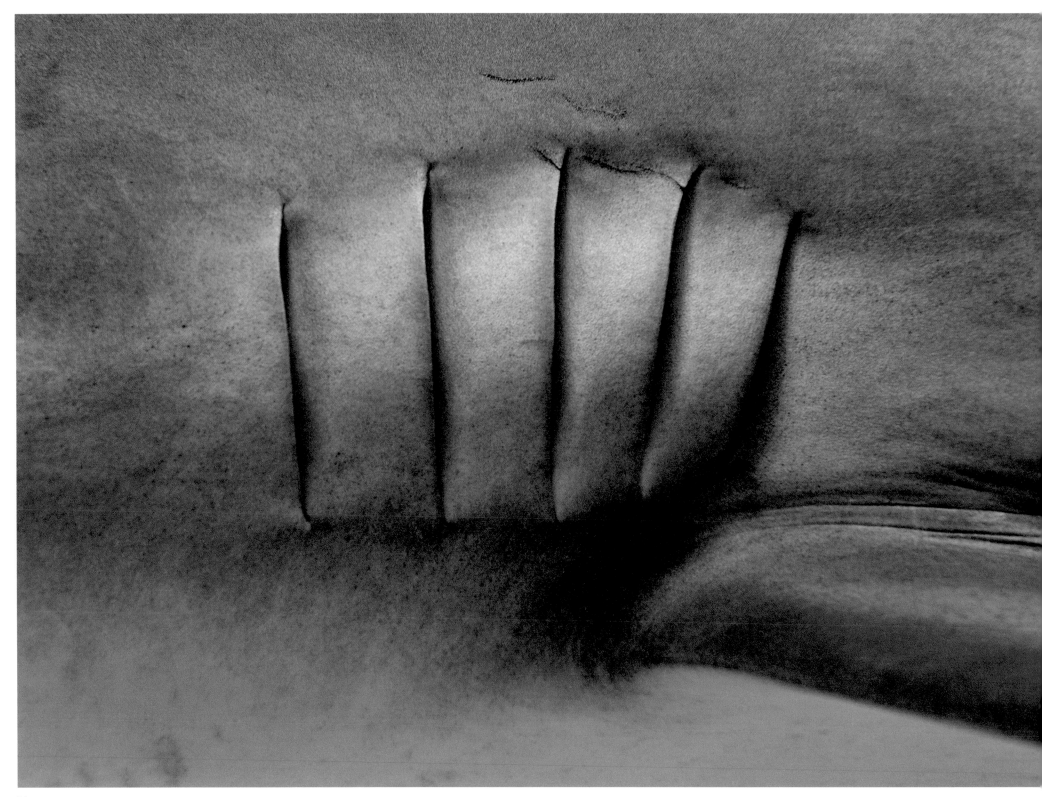

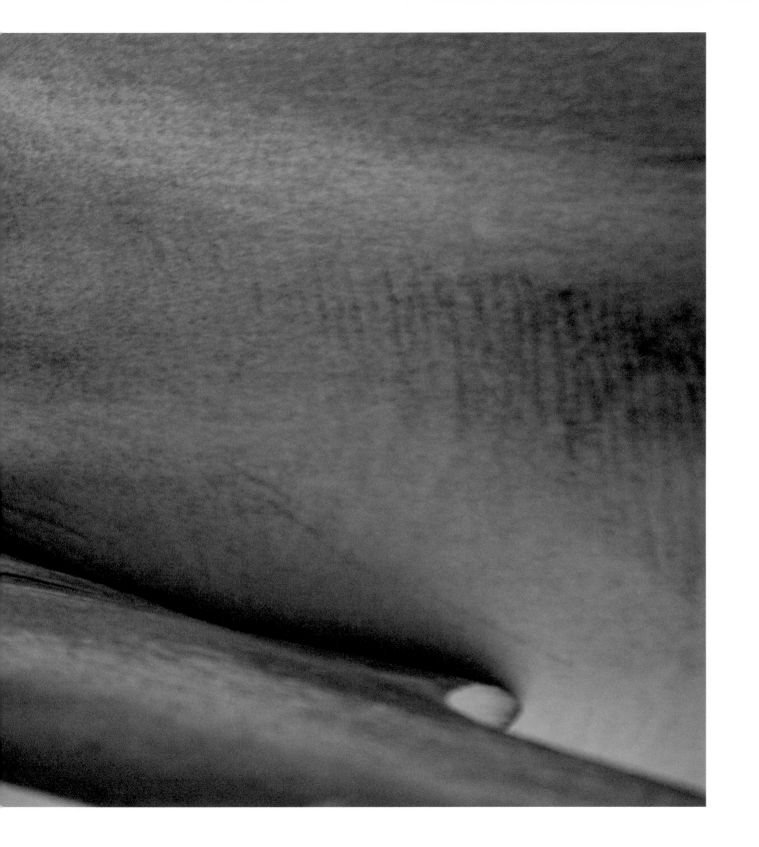

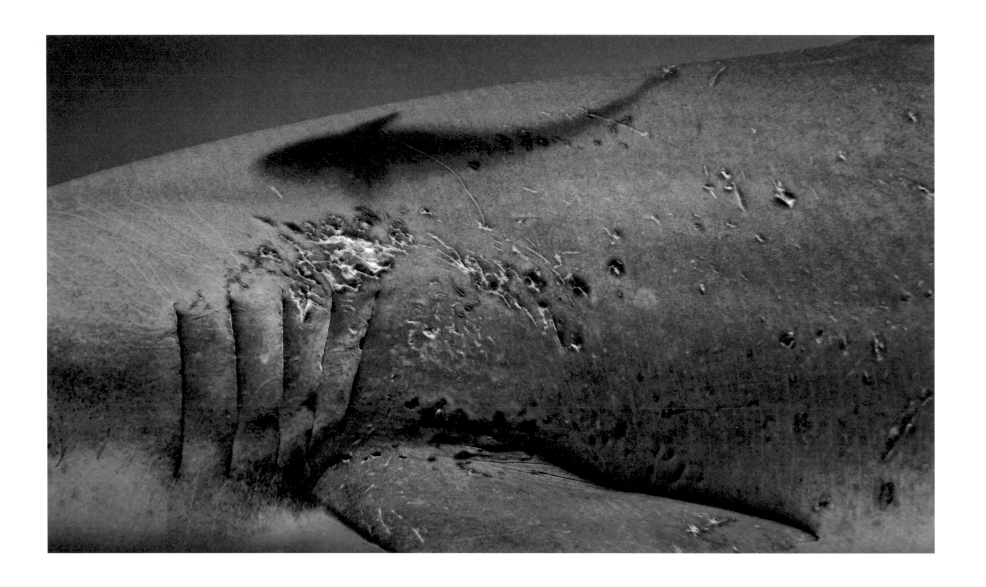

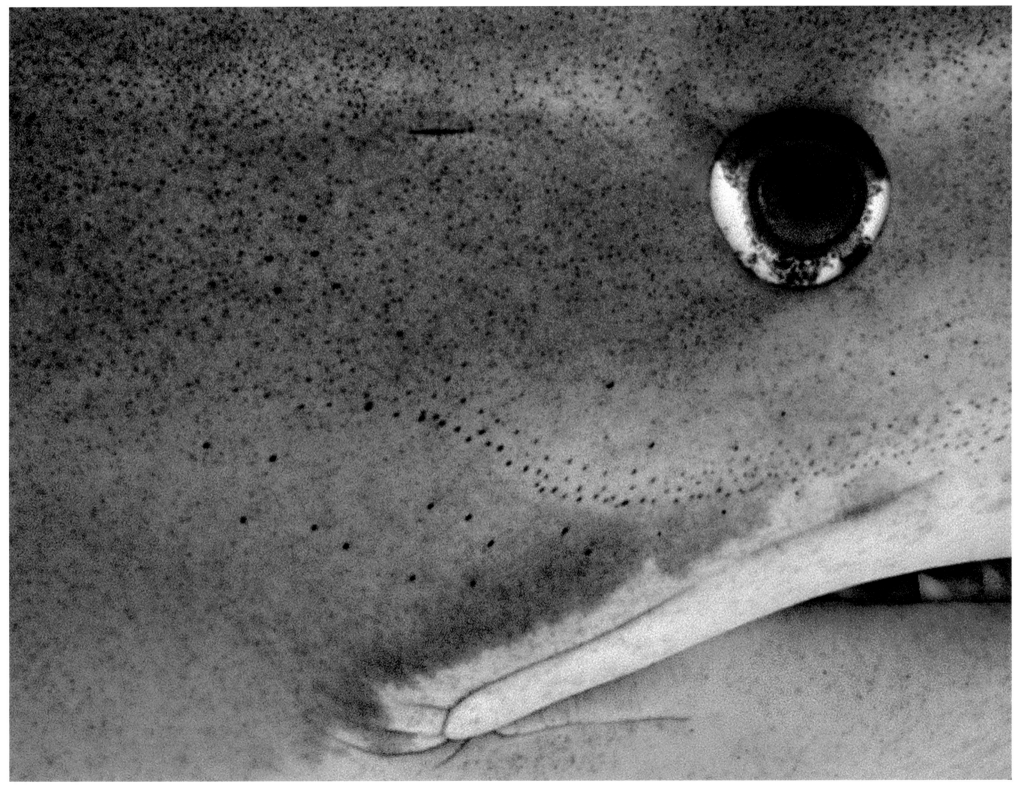

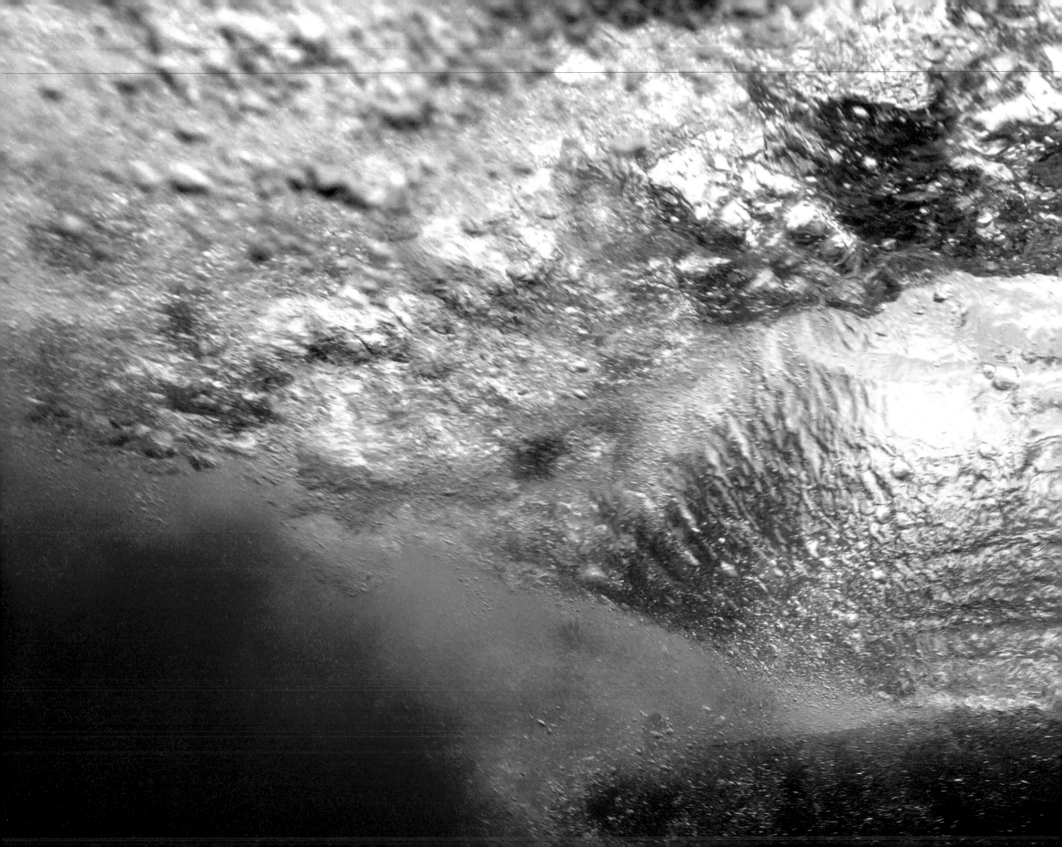

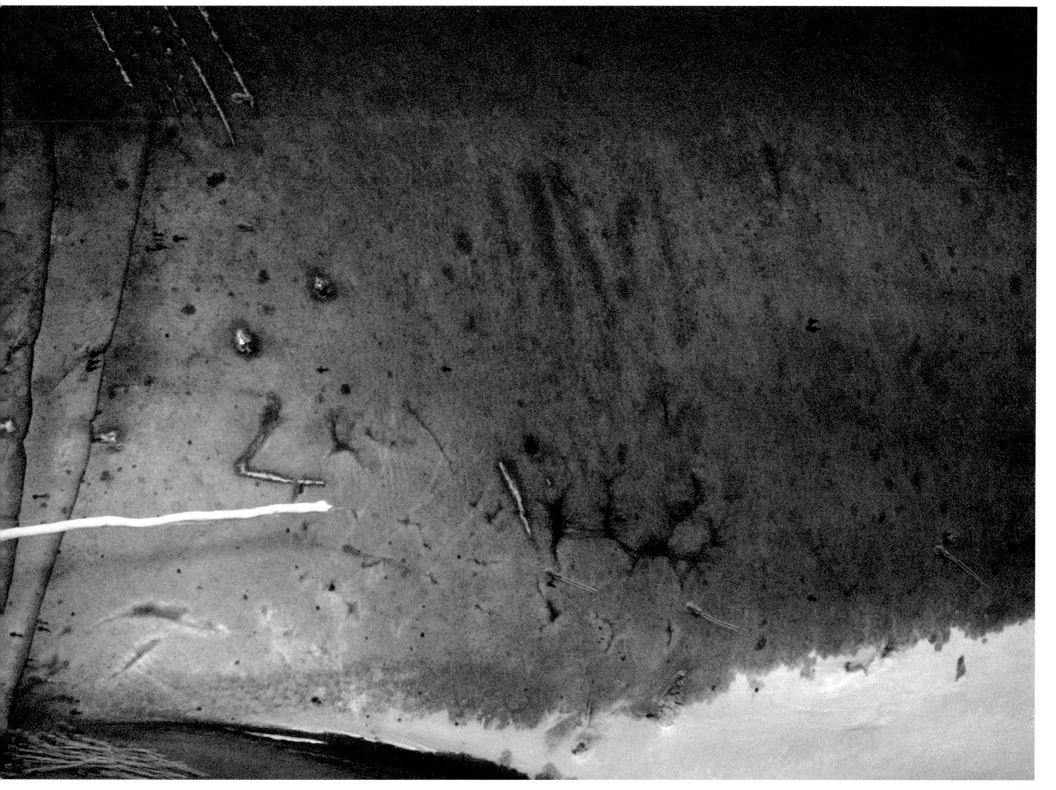

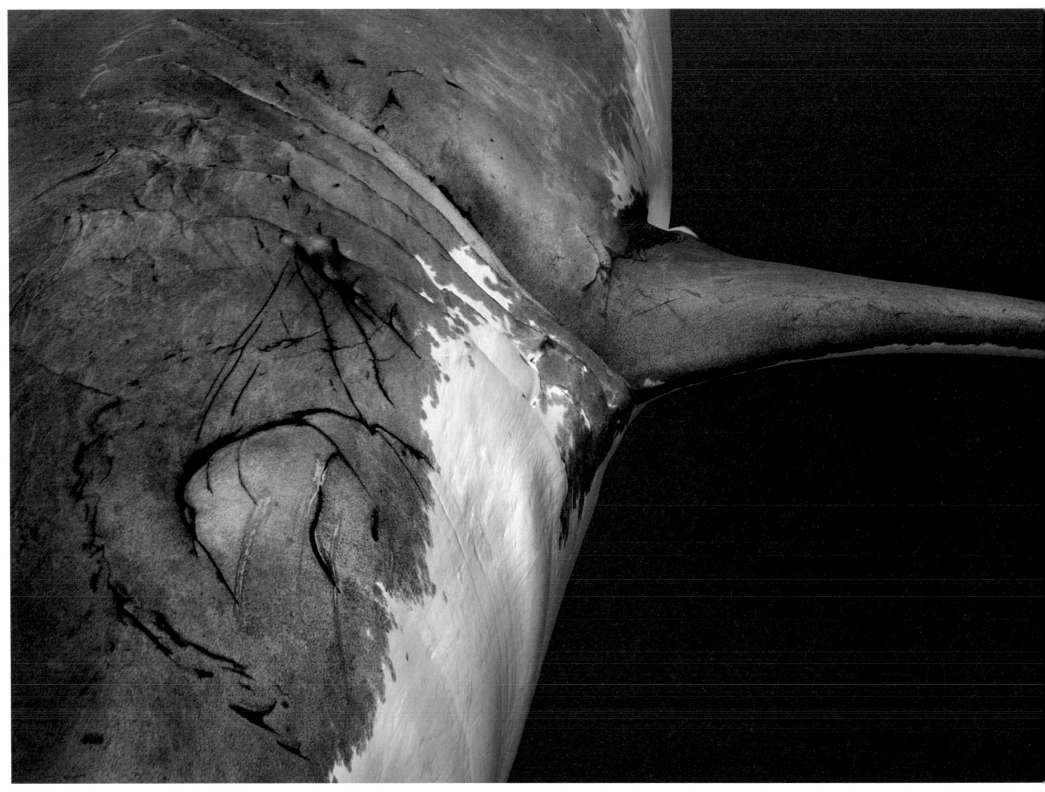

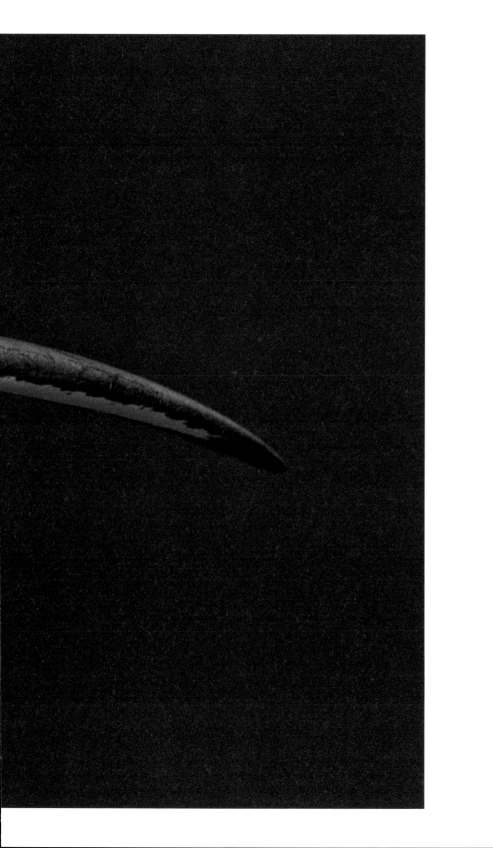

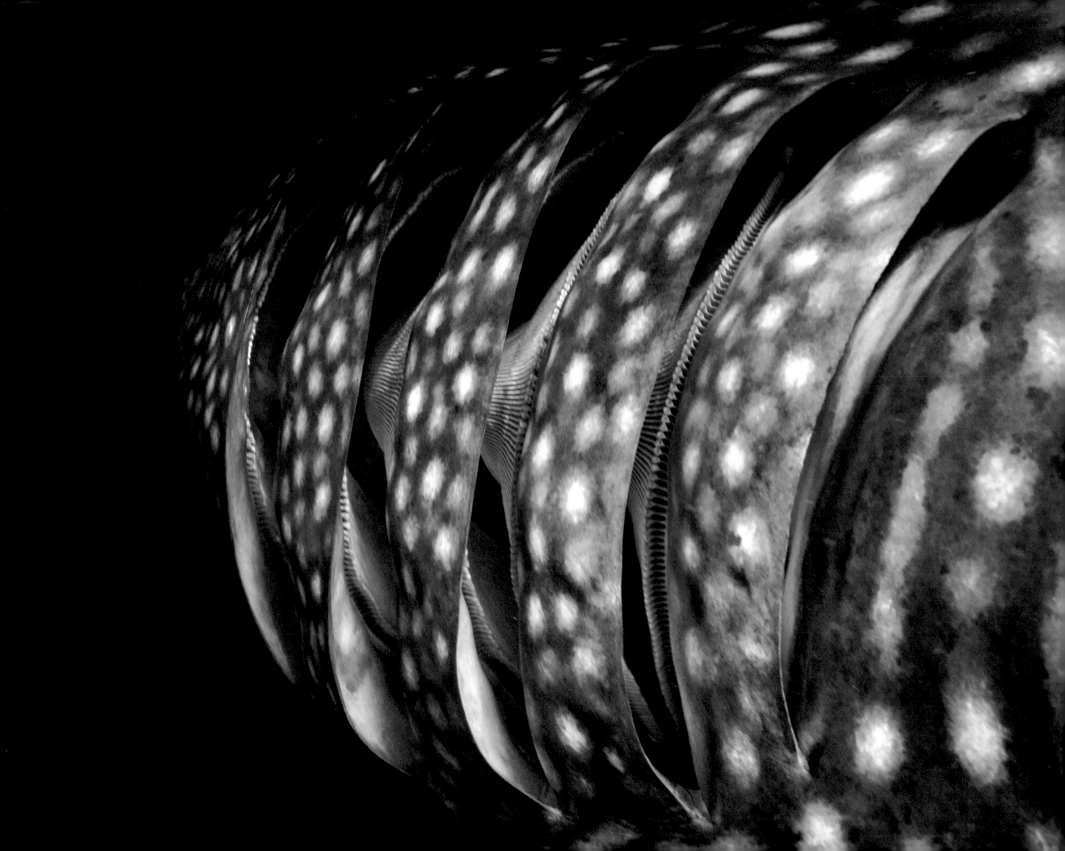

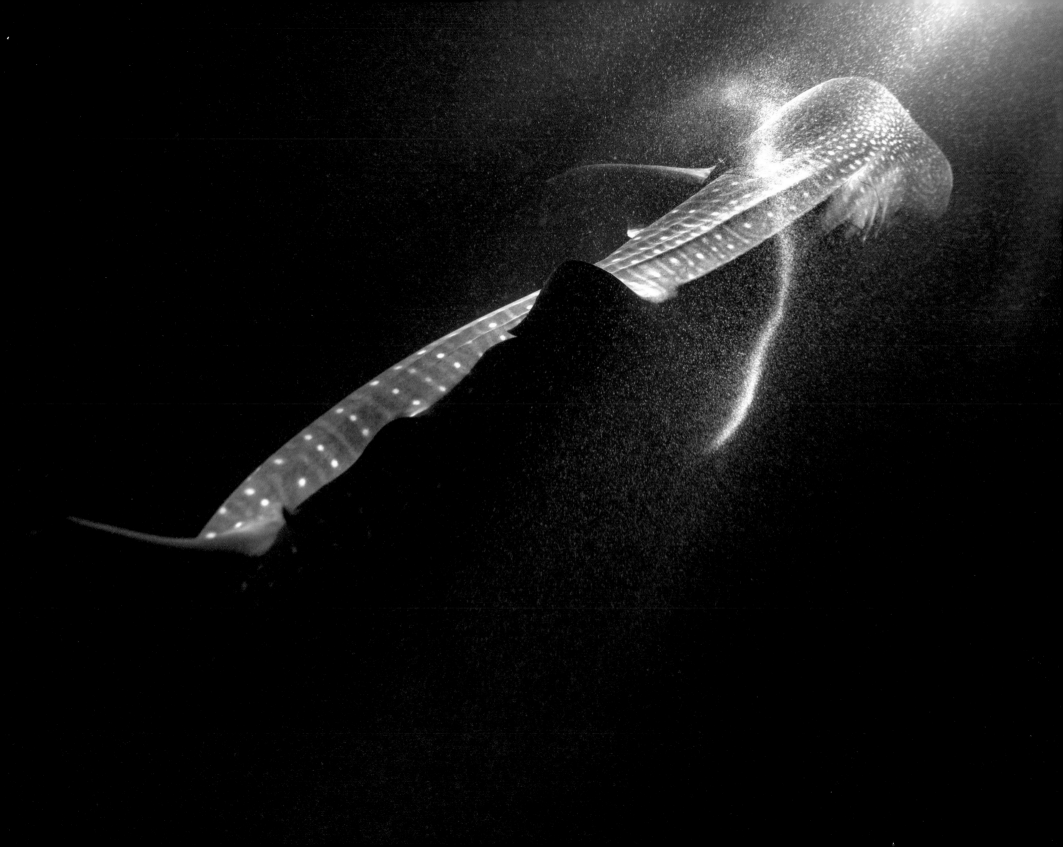

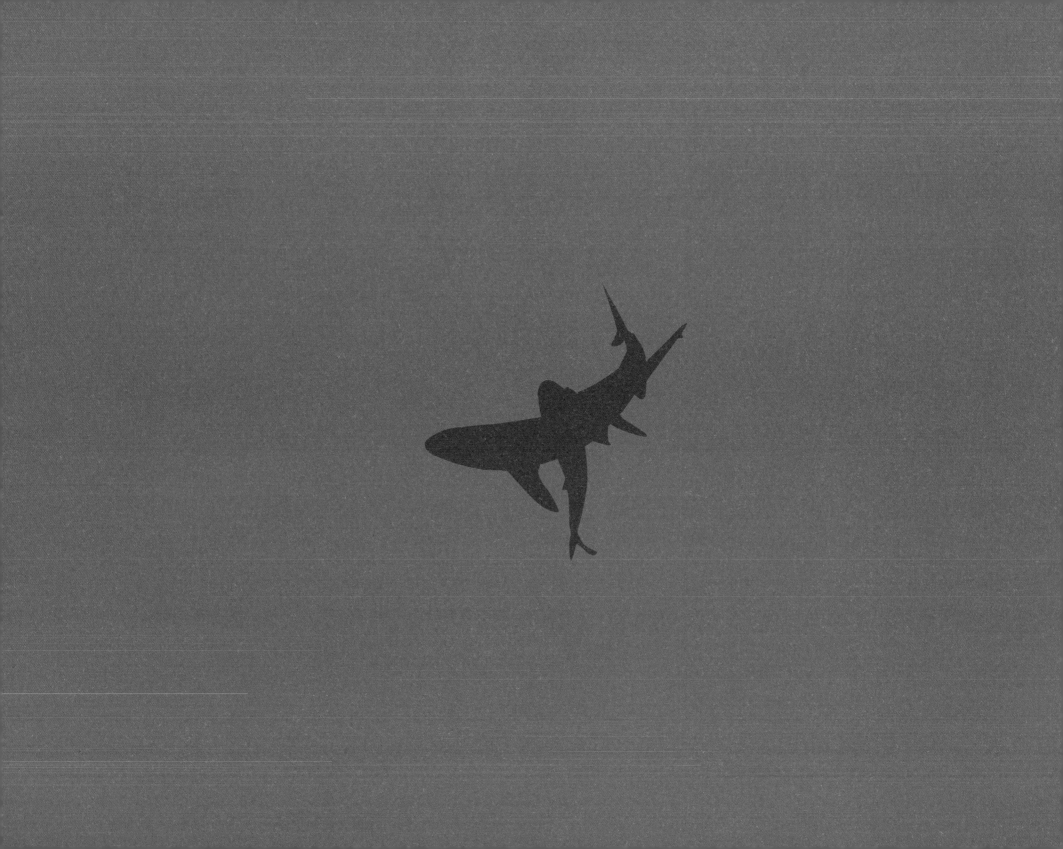

SHARK STORIES >>>

Page 5

OSPREY REEF

I have just barely intensified the density of the sky in the photograph, but the colours of the reef actually reflect reality. We are on board Mike Ball's boat preparing for a private shark feed – a poor choice of words since sharks are not fed so much as lured with bait in a plastic box. Violent winds and strong currents make it difficult for Hanli and Peter to stay upright 20 metres above the pinnacle where we are moored.

Australia, Osprey reef • August 2012
📷 14 mm • f 14 • 1/800

Page 8

THE CAST

I owe this photograph to Pablo, my first buddy. It was shot during an encounter with sharks off the Playa del Carmen. I owe Pablo so much more, since it was he who insisted – in Cala Vadella – that I should progressively overcome my fear of water and the difficulties I experienced in balancing the pressure in my ears and sinuses. It was Pablo who took me for my very first encounter with sharks off the coast of Mexico in January 2009.

Thank you my friend.

Page 9

FIRST ENCOUNTER

My first encounter. For decades, he has haunted every moment I have spent at sea. At last, I kneel before him at a depth of 30 metres, accompanied by four other divers. 'Time, suspend your flight.' Now I fully grasp the meaning of Lamartine's verse. Eternity, unity, a chosen moment amongst all others… revealing me to myself and inviting me to love this animal that symbolizes our collective fear.

Page 6

AN ADAPTED EYE
Prionace glauca

This young female blue shark tried to bite me a few seconds earlier. I easily got rid of her, gently pressing my thumb to her eye, hand flat on her head. No doubt frustrated by this failed attempt, she carries on misbehaving when she sees the other divers. Like all deep-sea sharks, she builds her reference system to know what food is right for her. She cannot really harm us if we don't give her the time to puncture our skin, by keeping ourselves constantly moving. The large eye of this species has grown to adapt to the weak light of the depths of its hunting ground.

South Africa, 70 km South of the Cape of Good Hope • July 2012
📷 70 mm • f 4.5 • 1/500

Page 10

THE JOURNEY BEGINS

January 2009: my thirty-fifth dive. At 53 years of age, I experienced this first encounter with unexpected intensity and serenity. This is not just any shark… The bull shark – seen on the right of the image – causes more fatal events than any other. The few images I brought back from this early dive still make me laugh to this day… I was so inexperienced that I'd taken a 3200 ASA film with me. I had no idea how much these images and encounters would change my life. Their naïve and childish character inspired me to write children's books and my technical mediocrity meant that I decided to use the best available equipment from the start. As for the sharks, it took just one dive to turn my visceral fear into a total, irrational, unconditional passion. The remora at the centre of the image still arouses curiosity as it hovers like a spaceship alongside all large marine animals.

Page 13

FEAR
Carcharhinus limbatus

Can beauty cure fear? How can we talk of a cure without speaking of the fear itself? A friend of mine once asked me this question and I wanted to find a way to symbolize it. In our collective unconscious, this fin breaking the surface of the water is the perfect illustration of our innermost fear. Just this once, I took the liberty of darkening the sky in the photograph to make the fin stand out more dramatically against the horizon.

South Africa, Haliwal Shoal • July 2011 📷 24 mm • f 11 • 1/500

RAIN AT SEA

During the sardine run, during which millions of sardines rush along the South African coast during the austral winter, the weather conditions often prove difficult, as is perfectly illustrated by this image of a typical rainy day. I was truly inspired by the sheer beauty of the elements and the unknown domain beneath the boat.

South Africa, Port St Johns • 📷 24 mm • f 7.1 • 1/200

CAREFUL...
Carcharhinus leucas

After more than a thousand hours spent with sharks, I still get a sense of mistrust around bull sharks. Commanding the fear of surfers and swimmers in areas close to river mouths, they move effortlessly from saltwater to freshwater, swimming upstream over improbable distances. They are also the most fearsome hunters in murky waters. Rarely on their own, the dominant member of the group strikes first, often followed by an opportunistic companion after the victim has been bitten. In more than fifty per cent of cases after being bitten victims lose blood quickly and die. They keep a safe distance from swimmers if they know they are being watched. Never turn your back on them.

Fiji, Pacific Harbour • March 2010 • 📷 18 mm • f 5.6 • 1/125

FROM THE SHARK'S POINT OF VIEW
Prionace glauca

Since the very beginning of my adventure with sharks, I have wondered how they perceive us. Throughout these four years, I tried to put myself in their place before judging their behaviour. This is how I understood the fact that divers look completely unfamiliar to a blue shark: the diver is vertical whereas almost all the other animals that it encounters in the ocean are horizontal. This alone is enough to justify a shark's curiosity.

South Africa, 70 km south of the Cape of Good Hope • July 2012
📷 62 mm • f 3.2 • 1/320

KLAUS AND THE WHITETIP SHARK
Carcharhinus longimanus

During a journey to Egypt in 2010, I met Klaus, an extraordinary 80-year-old man. Two years earlier, he had suffered a diving accident that left him temporarily deprived of the use of his legs. Klaus is an inveterate underwater photographer who wrote the first books on the Red Sea's flora and fauna and is one of its true discoverers. After having partially regained the use of his legs at the age of 79, he asked his doctor if he could start diving again. Faced with the physician's categorical refusal, he asked 'how about free diving?' The doctor burst out laughing but didn't say no...

In this image, Klaus returns to his first passion. I have seen him free diving to a depth of about 10 metres, something for which I envy him to this day. But it's never too late to start; it's just down to motivation...

Egypt, Daedalus • November 2010 • 📷 19 mm • f 6.3 • 1/160

A DAZZLING SPECTACLE
Carcharinus amblyrhynchos

More than 20 metres below the surface, they come and go on the current, moving effortlessly. This is one of the most beautiful sights of the world of sharks that I can remember. I found it very hard to do as my computer was telling me to return to the surface. The age-old myth of man-eating sharks was severely challenged that day: some 200 of the creatures passed no more than a few metres from us, with complete indifference.

French Polynesia, South Fakarava • March 2010
📷 24 mm • f 5.6 • 1/160

DIMPLE
Carcharhinus amblyrhynchos

I swam with sharks for more than one thousand hours before observing such tiny details as the precaudal dimple, which gives enhanced mobility to the sharks' tail, or their small precaudal fin... Absolute technological wonders.

French Polynesia, Rangiroa • February 2013 • 📷 60 mm • f 7 • 1/200

PERFECT GEOMETRY
Carcharhinus falciformis

The silky shark does not immediately approach the diver but chooses to wait for a moment of inattention. Seen in the Tuamotus, this specimen was by no means shy and kept me company for the entire duration of the dive, allowing me to admire his perfect geometry.

French Polynesia, Rangiroa • February 2013
📷 70 mm • f 9 • 1/125   📷 70 mm • f 6.3 • 1/160

THE MARKS OF TIME
Carcharinus albimarginatus

We are close to the shelf break in the Tiputa Pass. Two magnificent silvertip sharks dominate the scene. The grey reef sharks part as they slither through the waters. This shark is an adult male, as we can make out from the marks at the back of the eye. Strange analogy with man.

French Polynesia, Rangiroa • September 2010
📷 70 mm • f 7.1 • 1/200

FRENZY
Carcharhinus longimanus

We provoked a feeding frenzy in order to capture these very rapid, unusual movements by oceanic whitetip sharks. Our experience showed that it is extremely difficult to induce this reaction below a minimum number of four or five individuals.
The utmost caution is needed, since these sharks will seek the source of the olfactory signals in the flow cone and try to bite anything they find there. The risk of bites is very high if you find yourself near it during the triggering of the frenzy, which is over as quickly as it started after a very short period.

Egypt, Daedalus reef • November 2012
📷 24 mm • f 4 • 1/60

FRENZY
Carcharhinus amblyrhynchos

This image is doubly interesting. The grey reef shark carrying away the fish head in its jaws is blind. This is the second time I have witnessed greater initiative taken by sharks that are suffering from a physical handicap. The other interesting aspect to the image is that it shows that the presence of food inevitably results in a highly dynamic – even aggressive – attitude in a group of sharks, not dissimilar to that of a pack of dogs.

Australia, Osprey Reef • August 2012
📷 18 mm • f 5.6 • 1/125

THE MOBILE
Carcharhinus amblyrhynchos

They swirl around incessantly, attracted by the scent of the prey. This image is one of the first to fulfil my criteria for this book after more than one month travelling. I shot it in the late afternoon; the light is uniform but slightly lacks intensity. This is my first dive into the blue. It is unsettling, as I have no reference point and spend most of my time correcting my depth.

French Polynesia, Rangiroa • March 2010
📷 70 mm • f 5 • 1/100

A COUPLE IN HARMONY
Carcharhinus amblyrhynchos

I never imagined that I would ever capture this sort of image of sharks. It seemed to me only dolphins could move with such harmony and grace. As I witnessed their graceful movements, I knew I had to reveal this dance that they performed, giving us the greatest pleasure.

French Polynesia, Rangiroa • March 2010   📷 70 mm • f 4.5 • 1/80

FAMILY PORTRAIT
Carcharhinus amblyrhynchos

In the blue water, the awareness of your position in space quickly disappears as you concentrate on maintaining the same depth. These grey reef sharks dance tirelessly. I had to stay at a distance to capture these images, entering the group and slowly swimming a little higher to take advantage of the rays of afternoon light filtering through 15 metres of water. Beneath the sharks, several hundred metres of water lend homogeneity to the background. To capture these magical seconds, I tried to watch these sharks with the eyes of a child, wide open in a perpetual quest for a few moments of harmony.

French Polynesia • February 2011   📷 36 mm • f 5.6 • 1/125

SARAH AND THE TIGER
Galeocerdo cuvier

The star of the show is not the one you might expect. Look to the bottom right of the image. This was 23-year-old Sarah's first dive since she obtained her open water qualification. She fearlessly accompanied us on this impressive adventure. We are 20 metres below the surface while bull sharks come and go before us. We managed to count around thirty, some of which are over 4 metres long. Suddenly, the sharks disappear. We know that something's up, but Sarah can't believe her eyes when she sees a magnificent female tiger shark moving back and forth in front of her.

For safety's sake, a diver armed with a shark-billy (a protective stick) was positioned behind Sarah, who later told us that she did not feel scared at any time during the dive. This was also my first encounter with a tiger shark. I did not for a moment realize just how much I would grow to love this species.

Fiji, Pacific Harbour • March 2010 📷 24 mm • f 6.3 • 1/160

MASTER OF THE SHELF BREAK
Galeocerdo cuvier

A hierarchy is soon established. Other species near the bait know this. As soon as a tiger shark draws near and long before we catch a glimpse of it, they have already swum away. We can see them in the background, a good distance away from their potential predator. The mid-afternoon light gives incredible relief to this tiger shark that rules as the undefeated master of the shelf break.

French Polynesia, Rangiroa • March 2011 📷 24 mm • f 4.5 • 1/200

HEAD IN THE CORAL
Galeocerdo cuvier

Yves, Dominique and I had patiently to endure long sessions with our rebreathers on the outer reef waiting for a visit from this tiger shark. Excited by the tuna head bait, the shark did not hesitate to plunge its nose into the coral in its attempt to find it.

French Polynesia, Rangiroa • March 2011 📷 28 mm • f 4.5 • 1/60

NOT A RIPPLE
Carcharhinus melanopterus

I waited a long time to capture this image, simply because I wanted the sharks to forget about me. I'm standing up to my knees in the water in Tetamanu Village. The sharks come and go, not too far away from me. Then this blacktip reef shark decides to explore a few feet away from me, not making a single ripple on the surface of the shallow water (no deeper than 40 centimetres at most). Hail to the champion of silent swimming!

French Polynesia, South Fakarava • March 2013 📷 24 mm • f 11 • 1/500

BIZARRE ONE TO ONE
Sphyrna mokarran

Which of these strange creatures comes from another world? Yves, wearing a rebreather and armed with his camera casing, seems less well adapted to his environment than this great hammerhead. In this strange one to one, technology doesn't have the final say.

French Polynesia, Rangiroa • March 2011 📷 50 mm • f 4.5 • 1/200

THE CLOWN
Sphyrna mokarran

Near the shelf break after a 3-hour dive using a recycler in Rangiroa, we met this female great hammerhead. Her clown-like appearance startled us, and I managed to photograph her during these few stolen seconds in the late afternoon light. Sometimes you just need a tiny bit of luck to enjoy perfect shooting conditions. That's when the magic works best.

French Polynesia, Rangiroa • March 2011 📷 70 mm • f 4 • 1/160

STARTLED GREAT HAMMERHEAD
Sphyrna mokarran

In just ten days, we spent more than thirty hours on a rebreather – a self-contained breathing apparatus – waiting for this great hammerhead at the break of the outer slope of the Rangiroa lagoon. My hurried approach prompted an immediate reaction. I wanted to shoot a close-up of his eye. Needless to say that I didn't get it… The shark's posture speaks volumes as to the muscular presence he can bring to bear, and it's easy to understand why other sharks move on whenever he comes near.

French Polynesia, Rangiroa • February 2013 📷 38 mm • f 4 • 1/160

THE ROSE GARDEN
Carcharhinus amblyrhynchos

During a drift dive at more than 5 km/h in the northern pass of Fakarava, we glide over the rose garden and meet a grey reef shark swimming against the current. In this stolen image, the black and white tones heighten the contrast between the various different surfaces.

French Polynesia, North Fakarava • March 2010
📷 66 mm • f 5.6 • 1/125

THE PREDATORS' CLUB
Carcharhinus albimarginatus

This strange crew is made up of jacks rubbing against a silvertip shark. To what end? Do they want to take advantage of the roughness of the shark's skin to remove parasites or are they teasing him to chase him away? This photo was taken at the end of the day, at the exit of the Tikehau pass.

French Polynesia, Tikehau • February 2013
📷 66 mm • f 7 • 1/200

OLD SHARK
Triaenodon obesus

There's no mistaking the age of this old whitetip reef shark. Its gills have collapsed and we can clearly distinguish the lines and bags around its eyes. Note the round scar typical of the bite of the cookiecutter shark (*Isistius brasiliensis*). Measuring only fifty centimetres, this type of shark bites off morsels of flesh to feed and will attack any prey, including whales, dolphins and sharks. A few night divers have experienced cookiecutter shark attacks, suffering considerable deep tissue damage

French Polynesia, Tikehau • February 2013
📷 62 mm • f 9 • 1/320

SURVIVOR
Alopias pelagicus

Meeting this beautiful thresher shark on the edge of the shelf break was the only truly beautiful moment of this second journey to Daedalus. Following my wonderful experience with oceanic whitetip sharks the previous year, Hanli and I decided to go and meet them. However, we had not considered the reprisals following several alleged shark attacks near Sharm-el-Sheikh, and all oceanic whitetip sharks had been eradicated. I have rarely felt such anger and sadness. There were sixteen of us on the boat. None of us saw a single shark during that entire week.

With a heavy heart, I decided to dive alone whilst the others took a nap and I went down to 40 metres. I met a grouper and started taking photographs. Suddenly a shadow appeared in the frame. I couldn't believe my eyes. The shark came right at me. I held my breath for a minute, afraid of scaring him, and managed to take a series of shots in the clear water. When I returned to the boat, no one believed that I had met a thresher. They had to see it for themselves. Although I broke basic safety rules, my perseverance was duly rewarded.

Egypt, Daedalus • September 2011 📷 70 mm • f 5 • 1/100

FINS
Carcharhinus albimarginatus

You have to really want to know all about sharks to observe the working of these fins. You mustn't be afraid to get extremely close to these animals, which proves very difficult since sharks consider this behaviour as an attempt at predation and often pick up speed in order to put some distance between them and you.

French Polynesia, Rangiroa • February 2013
📷 70 mm • f 7.1 • 1/200   📷 70 mm • f 8.1 • 1/250

SHY AND RETIRING
Alopias pelagicus

First leg of the journey: Malapscua, the Philippines. I chose this location because it's probably the best place on earth to meet the pelagic thresher shark and local guides 'guarantee' an encounter for every dive. After two dives a day for a week, I had only glimpsed one distant shape in the milky waters. At the end of this first great journey, three months later, I finally shot this picture near the cleaning station.

This meeting touched me deeply, as the thresher shark is timid and distant. You need patience or luck if you want to take great photos. Its gaze is reminiscent of a frightened animal and its wide eyes reinforce the impression that you are looking at a cartoon character. It has a particularly long tail – as long as the rest of its body – that it uses like a whip to stun its prey before catching them, and also to help it leap out of the water to get rid of parasites.

Philippines, Malapascua • April 2010 📷 48 mm • f 4 • 1/60

STEVE AND THE BIRDS

On a wonderfully stormy day during the sardine run, as we were looking for hunting scenes, we realized that the birds were extremely intrigued by our presence. To test their curiosity, Steve went into the water and, a few seconds later, these three birds came to see him as if to say 'what on earth are you doing in the water in this weather?' Steve had to be very careful of the sharks lurking below the surface which had no qualms about taking advantage of the poor underwater visibility to approach his diving fins.

South Africa, Port St Johns • July 2011 📷 56 mm • f 11 • 1/400

HANLI AND THE BLUE SHARK
Prionace glauca

We had been at sea for almost two hours and had lost sight of the Cape of Good Hope. Here, there is a real danger of drifting and losing sight of the boat, as the current is significant and the swell quickly hides a diver coming up to the surface. This young blue shark let Hanli approach and accompany him for a while. Like all other deep-sea sharks, blue sharks quickly come into contact with divers to identify any 'object' roaming in their territory. This shark owes its name to the bluish sheen of its skin on the upper part of its body.

South Africa, 60 km to the south of the Cape of Good Hope • January 2012
📷 14 mm • f 5 • 1/640

GREAT FRIENDS
Carcharhinus limbatus

This blacktip shark seems to possess a metallic-looking fairing. Isolating the specimen from the group proved difficult, particularly as we needed a clear background and had to wait for the right moment to illustrate this cohabitation. We are at Aliwal Shoal during the austral winter, 10 metres below the surface. Turbidity ensures a greater homogeneity for the background as the water column somewhat dims the light, thus bringing softness to the image.

South Africa, Aliwal Shoal • January 2010 📷 58 mm • f 7 • 1/200

THE SHARK'S DECISION
Carcharhinus limbatus

The shark responds immediately to Hanli's gesture. In a split second, it moves so that she cannot touch it, as we can see in its body's dynamic. Hanli hasn't had time to shift her body position or even to follow it with her eyes. The shark alone decides whether an interaction will take place… or not.

South Africa, Aliwal Shoal • July 2011 📷 15 mm • f 6.3 • 1/640

TRUST
Carcharhinus longimanus

This image best symbolizes the reconciliation between man and shark. Displaying its trust through its relaxed mouth as the nictitating membrane – or third protecting eyelid – clears its eye, the shark shows that it does not feel threatened by the presence of a hand resting on it. It took several days of contact with this group of oceanic whitetips before this scene was possible. Martin let this shark come and go as it pleased until a delicate, non-intrusive moment of physical contact took place. From then on, the shark actively sought such contact… and this is the result.

Egypt, Daedalus reef • November 2010 📷 20 mm • f 5 • 1/100

STYLE CONTEST
Carcharhinus limbatus

These figures compete for the first prize for elegance. The blacktip shark has no intention of letting Hanli get too close.

South Africa, Aliwal Shoal • July 2011
📷 17 mm • f 5.6 • 1/500

ENOUGH FOR EVERYONE
Carcharhinus limbatus

There's something offbeat about this shot. While Hanli bends her head, pinching her nose to balance the internal pressure, a remora looks for a place where it can stick its new friend. Meanwhile, the shark is already carrying a free rider.

South Africa, Aliwal Shoal • July 2011

RACING FINS
Carcharhinus limbatus

Many blacktip sharks have set up home near the Aliwal Shoal reef, offshore Umkomaas. In ten years, they have rapidly replaced other historic species and now dominate these waters.

Taken at the end of a dive, this image shows sharks hunting for sardines on the surface and exhibiting a behaviour that is not far off feeding frenzy. As you hold your vertical position in the water, it is imperative that you should remain calm, keeping your arms close to your body, with no shiny objects nearby. If you stick to these rules, everything should go well.

South Africa, Aliwal Shoal • July 2010 📷 24 mm • f 14 • 1/800

ABOUT-FACE
Prionace glauca

She's back! I have just pushed her away and here she comes again, nibbling Morne's valves and hood. My diving companion's face shows no fear; he even seems amused by the reaction of the blue shark. As Morne checks his control screen after photographing her, the shark decides to do an about-face and startle him. It is essential constantly to maintain visual contact with a shark, which will always keep its distance as long as it can look into your eyes.

South Africa, 70 km south of the Cape of Good Hope • July 2012 📷 24 mm • f 4.5 • 1/500

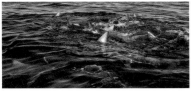

THE DANCE OF THE FINS
Carcharhinus limbatus

This image perfectly illustrates a feeding frenzy. Blacktip sharks fight over sardines near the surface. The winter light gives their coppery sheen a surrealist quality, the underwater silhouettes emphasizing the dramatic effect.
Although few accidents involve blacktip sharks, this image is unlikely to encourage divers into the water.

South Africa, Aliwal Shoal • July 2010 📷 30 mm • f 13 • 1/640

UNTIL THE VERY LAST ONE...
Carcharhinus limbatus

This peaceful image does not reflect the harsh reality that recurs every year in offshore South African waters during the sardine run, a major event during which countless sardines swim up the eastern coastline to Durban, thus providing their predators with an almost endless food supply. A blacktip shark waits for the next dolphin assault on the sardine shoal to get his share of the feast. This attack will provoke utter chaos and the 'ball' formation will prove useless for the doomed sardines, all of which will be mercilessly devoured.

South Africa, Port St Johns • July 2010 📷 24 mm • f 5.6 • 1/125

AWESOME AGILITY
Prionace glauca

This image testifies to the elegance and agility of these blue sharks swimming in the open sea. These incredibly quick animals can make a U-turn on the spot. I have been amazed by the swiftness of their movements on many occasions. I could not take my eyes off them.

South Africa, 70 km to the south of the Cape of Good Hope • July 2012 📷 70 mm • f 4.5 • 1/500

FINDING THE INTRUDER...
Carcharhinus limbatus

A split second elapsed between these two shots. The first image gives an idea of the dynamic generated when food is thrown to sharks. I hesitated for a long time before using the second image in this book, as it does not fulfil my usual criteria. I'd asked Hanli to swim back up to the surface and to swim next to one or two sharks. The sailor on board the boat nearby was eager to please me and tried to help out by throwing a few sardines into the water, almost on top of me. Of course the sharks rushed straight to me. For a split second, I thought that I would be bitten while the sharks jostled me. To this day, I still get flashbacks to the adrenaline rush I experienced. I looked for Hanli in the crowd. If you study the photograph carefully, you can see her hooded head at the centre of the second image. This is not an experience that I shall ever repeat.

As we climbed back on board, the sailor roared with laughter and simply asked me if I was pleased with the shots I'd taken. There was really nothing to add...

South Africa, Umkomaas • July 2011 📷 14 mm • f 5 • 1/250

BLUE SHARK AND DIVERS
Prionace glauca

The two figures in the background intrigued the shark, probably because the diver on the right was inexperienced. Morne suggested that she should encounter sharks in the deep sea but she didn't yet have the ability to control her depth. Still, she got out of the water with a huge smile on her face. Morne had to push away the blue sharks gently on several occasions.

South Africa, 70 km to the south of the Cape of Good Hope • January 2012 📷 24 mm • f 6.3 • 1/160

MYSTERIES OF THE KELP FOREST
Notorynchus cepedianus

This image requires careful attention from the viewer. The main characters are hard to make out at first: seen from this angle, Hanli could be part of the vegetation and you really have to look closely to find the three broad nose sevengill sharks plunged in the 'mist'. This is an invitation to dream and travel if ever you find yourself in Cape Town.

South Africa, Miles Point • July 2011 📷 24 mm • f 4 • 1/250

UNDERWATER OUTING
Notorynchus cepedianus

A morning outing in the cold waters at Miles Point. Hanli and this broadnose sevengill shark seem to share the landscape harmoniously. In these surreal surroundings, time has stopped for our heroes. We are struck by the violent contrast between one of the marine world's most ancient species and this sci-fi figure.

South Africa, Miles Point • April 2011
📷 14 mm • f 5 • 1/100

ENCOUNTERS IN THE KELP FOREST
Notorynchus cepedianus

At my request, Hanli lets herself float, eyes looking up towards the surface. In less than a minute, an inquisitive Broadnose sevengill shark comes to greet her. In the background, a second shark can be seen approaching. That morning, a particularly strong swell rolls Hanli from side to side.

South Africa, Miles Point • April 2011 📷 17 mm • f 4.5 • 1/80

Same place, three months later. The swell is just as powerful and Hanli still intrigues the sharks as she lies on the sea bed.

South Africa, Miles Point • July 2011 📷 14 mm • f 2.8 • 1/125

TWO EXTRA GILLS
Notorynchus cepedianus

Less than an hour away from Cape Town, we stray from our planned course and enter a fairytale world. The broadnose sevengill shark (most sharks have five gills) lives in the kelp forest. Today, the visibility is extraordinary. Usually it doesn't exceed 2 or 3 metres. Sharks appear and disappear as they please like so many strange vessels. Their almond-shaped eyes, simultaneously intense and serene, like golden flames, invite us to greet them.

South Africa, Miles Point • July 2011 📷 24 mm • f 3.2 • 1/160

HANLI AND THE KELP FOREST
Notorynchus cepedianus

Kelp forests, favoured by sevengill sharks, would belong in any fairy tale. Everything contributes to the sense of mystery: the turbid water, the nonchalance of passing sharks and the luxurious vegetation of giant seaweed. On the downside, as the water temperature only reaches 9 degrees centigrade that day, Hanli will only venture down a few times from the surface to the forest. Whenever she comes out of the water, Steve runs hot water in her wetsuit and gives her an obligatory hot chocolate.

South Africa, Simon's Town • April 2011 📷 24 mm • f 3.5 • 1/60

SURVIVOR
Carcharhinus amblyrhynchos

A fishing net left its mark in the network of scars running across the body of this grey reef shark. It is very lucky to be alive, as sharks quickly suffocate when they can't move.

French Polynesia, Rangiroa • February 2013
📷 35 mm • f 6.3 • 1/160

HANLI AND THE SAND TIGER SHARKS
Carcharias taurus

There is a dive site here known as the Cathedral, at a depth of more than 15 metres below the surface. The sharks spend their days there and hunt at night. Hanli is completely relaxed around them, to the point that she feels able to turn her back on them. The darkness in the background gives an idea of the depth of this cave that opens towards the surface via a chimney. Although visibility is rarely ideal, this is a beautiful diving spot.

South Africa, Aliwal Shoal • July 2011 📷 24 mm • f 4 • 1/60

Pages 90 & 91

STORM WARNINGS

After a difficult morning going out to sea, we endured the effects of the storm throughout the entire day. There was a 3-metre swell and underwater visibility was no more than 2 or 3 metres. Although I only stayed in the water for fifteen minutes the curiosity of these birds resulted in an image that would not be out of place in a thriller.

As I was treading water to take this photograph, I saw the dark shape of a shark at the tip of my diving fins. I still recall the deep sensation of insecurity I felt and I remember spending more time looking below the surface than above it to take my photos. I'd like to thank Steve for these unforgettable moments.

South Africa, Port St Johns • July 2011 • 📷 27 mm • f 14 • 1/800

Page 93

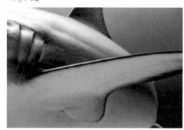

LIGHT TOUCH
Carcharhinus perezii

This image is taken with the human eye's focal length, as the shark softly brushes against me and I have just enough time to focus.

Bahamas, Nassau • June 2013
📷 56 mm • f 5.6 • 1/320

Pages 94 & 95

RIDING UPSIDE DOWN
Negaprion brevirostris

 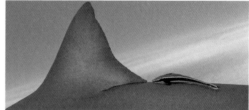

Remoras of all sizes accompany lemon sharks as they roam the waters of Tiger Beach. It is almost impossible to take a picture of a shark without one. With a sucker on their head, remoras spend most of their lives upside down. When they find themselves without their habitual vehicle, they can often be found trying to catch a ride on the legs of inattentive divers.

Bahamas, Tiger Beach • December 2013 📷 70 mm • f 8 • 1/125 📷 62 mm • f 8 • 1/250

Pages 96 & 97

FIVE, SIX, SEVEN...
Carcharhinus perezii

Although most sharks have five gills, a few species have six or seven. This highly sensitive area of the shark's body will prove useful if you want to put some distance between you and an intrusive shark. Hand held vertically, simply press the water towards the gills. The shark will immediately perceive the pressure change through its lateral lines and will prudently swim away.

Bahamas, Nassau • June 2013
📷 58 mm • f 5.6 • 1/500

Page 99

FIGHTER JET
Negaprion brevirostris

This lemon shark looks like a fighter jet with the remoras attached to it like weapons systems, making it look even more menacing.

Bahamas, Tiger Beach • October 2013 📷 70 mm • f 8 • 1/250

Page 100

FLOATING FIN
Carcharhinus perezii

This image allows us perfectly to differentiate a shark fin, the rear portion of which 'floats', from that of a dolphin or other cetaceans, where the fin is connected to the body along its full length.

Bahamas, Nassau • June 2013 📷 32 mm • f 5.6 • 1/320

LATERAL LINE AND LEADING EDGE
Carcharhinus perezii

This image illustrates two crucial mechanisms. On the one hand, we can make out the dots of the lateral line extending along the length of the shark's body. These pressure transmitters detect the slightest movement in the water, including the frantic thrashing of a wounded fish. The wave transmitted is immediately detected and interpreted as an opportunity. On the other hand, we can see the sinusoidal aspect of the tail's leading edge optimizing the water flow.

Bahamas, Nassau • June 2013 📷 58 mm • f 4 • 1/250

LET THE SHOW BEGIN!
Carcharhinus perezii

Reef sharks perform an infinite range of pirouettes, as though on a stage. The white sand clearing in the middle of the underwater vegetation further accentuates this effect.

Bahamas, Nassau • June 2013
📷 16 mm • f 4.5 • 1/320

CLEANER FISH
Carcharhinus perezii

I was photographing Martin as he 'charmed' his sharks when this unusual scene caught my eye. I only had time to zoom in and to shoot before the remora immediately reclaimed its position beneath the shark's belly. In more than one thousand hours spent in the company of sharks, this is the first time I had witnessed a remora cleaning parasites from a shark. The posture of this reef shark characterizes this sort of situation: he slows down, tilts to a 45 degree angle and opens his mouth to allow the fish to clean away parasites or food waste.

Bahamas, Nassau • June 2013 📷 70 mm • f 6.3 • 1/160

SCRAMBLE
Carcharhinus perezii

Martin is glad that he put on his chain mail suit. In just under an hour, a female shark bit him three times, apparently mistaking him for a feeder she didn't like… Each time, she took advantage of Martin's inattention to bite him. He emerged from this sticky situation almost intact, with just a few bruises and a single drop of blood under his chain mail suit. Whenever Martin takes a piece of bait from the metal container, a scramble ensues, and he is literally covered in sharks.

Bahamas, Nassau • June 2013 📷 18 mm • f 5 • 1/200

YAWNING SHARK
Carcharhinus perezii

Following a tropical storm, the atmosphere was very strange. The water was cloudy and the light was changing with the sky. This reef shark yawned a few yards away from my vantage point, probably to relax the articulation of its jaws. No prey in sight, no little cleaner fish around.

Bahamas, Nassau • June 2013
📷 32 mm • f 4 • 1/640

TONIC IMMOBILIZATION
Carcharhinus perezii

Martin spent 5 or 6 hours achieving his goal: putting a shark into tonic immobility. Not all sharks will allow this. Martin does not force the reef shark, but lets him put its nose in his hand as he delicately strokes it before taking hold of its dorsal fin as soon as the shark blinks, a sign of tonic immobility. The gentle stimulation of the ampullae of Lorenzini – the shark's electroreceptors – brings on this cataleptic state.

Bahamas, Nassau • June 2013 📷 20 mm • f 5 • 1/250

CHOREOGRAPHY
Carcharhinus perezii

This moment is intense. We set it up by burying a dead fish in the sand to study a feeding frenzy. Very soon, other fishes sense the dead one and attract the attention of reef sharks who come to fight over it.

The resulting dynamic is astonishing: the sharks twist and turn sharply violently, and the whole thing is breathtaking in its beauty and power.

I picked the location and waited for the right light to 'stage' this image. After three days of bad weather, the water's turbidity was high. I chose a spot of sand surrounded by greenery and waited for a cloud to pass overhead in order to achieve a more diffuse, homogeneous image. The shadows contribute to close up the image.

Bahamas, Nassau • June 2013
📷 24 mm • f 5.6 • 1/500

Page 111

THE LEMON SHARK'S PILOT FISH
Negaprion brevirostris

A pilot fish swims ahead of a lemon shark with prominent ampullae of Lorenzini – these electroreceptors are directly linked to the central nervous system and allow sharks to move in relation to the terrestrial electromagnetic field and to detect their prey, even in complete darkness.

Bahamas, Tiger Beach • June 2013 📷 70 mm • f 11 • 1/500

Page 112

70 mm • f 10 • 1/400

A REMORA'S SHADOW
Negaprion brevirostris

A swift movement of the lemon shark and the remora comes unstuck whilst its shadow is still visible. It soon returns to its favourite place. Traces of the shark's prenuptial bites can still be seen clearly.

Bahamas, Tiger Beach • June 2013 📷

Page 113

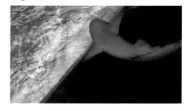

HIDDEN UNDERBELLIES
Negaprion brevirostris

When the camera finds an unusual angle, both the lemon shark and the boat reveal their underbellies at once.

Bahamas, Tiger Beach • June 2013
📷 56 mm • f 11 • 1/500

Page 115

TENDER GAZE
Galeocerdo cuvier

Why look for ferocity? This baby tiger shark is only 2.5 metres long and feels so intimidated by the presence of adult lemon sharks that I only managed to shoot one photograph. I immediately fell under the spell of his eyes, although he kept his distance for the entire duration of the dive. His outline was ever-present on the very edge of my field of vision.

Bahamas, Tiger Beach • June 2013 📷 70 mm • f 9 • 1/320

Pages 116 & 117

EMMA AND RENÉ
Galeocerdo cuvier

Emma, a beautiful tiger shark who has lived in the waters around the Bahamas for many years, proved very curious and came to us easily. Although she approached us very slowly, the experience remained incredibly impressive. I lay face down on the sea bed to take this photograph, as I wanted to be on the same level as her so that you could feel her presence. She saw me from some distance away and, completely relaxed, moved towards me. When she was a metre away, I knelt on the sand and put down my camera casing, holding out my open hands. She lay on my hands and I gently stroked her. René Heurey was filming the scene and probably enjoyed it as much as I did, as Emma went to him a few times. The fish on Emma's left looks as though he is confiding in her or suggesting that she should intimidate me in some way.

Bahamas, Tiger Beach • June 2013 📷 70 mm • f 8 • 1/250

Pages 118 & 119

RELATIONSHIP WITH A WILD ANIMAL
Galeocerdo cuvier

When I asked Leina to accompany me to the Bahamas, I wanted to take a very specific shot. This approach is unusual for me; in general I make do with what nature has to offer. Yet, revisiting all the images of inter-species encounters, I had observed that humans almost establish an unconscious hierarchical relationship in relation to the animal. This is the case for most of the previous images in this book. I wanted to capture a moment that would restore order in this situation; an invitation to an egalitarian relationship between man and shark. Who better than a woman to incarnate the role of the 'new man'?

Due to lack of time, I only managed to take this one shot but I think that it comes very close to the goal I'd had in mind, thanks to Leina's sincere openness to the shark. Thank you Leina. The sunspot further accentuates their presence at the border of the boat's shadow.

Bahamas, Tiger Beach • June 2013 📷 24 mm • f 10 • 1/400

Page 121

PORTRAIT OF A YOUNG TIGER
Galeocerdo cuvier

This young tiger shark and travelling companions swirl before my eyes in ideal lighting conditions. The slightly cloudy sky and pale background reflect the light, illuminating the shark's belly. Better than in a studio… where incidentally, I have never worked for a single day.

Bahamas, Tiger Beach • December 2013
📷 48 mm • f 8 • 1/250

Pages 122, 123 & 127

HANLI AND THE TIGER
Galeocerdo cuvier

Anyone who wishes to experience a fantastic adventure should visit the Bahamas. It is the ideal location for finding plenty of sharks, allowing for some great encounters. The waters are shallow, turbidity perfect and the light idyllic. The current, which can prove troublesome, is the only downside.

Bahamas, Tiger Beach • December 2013 📷 24 mm • f 9 • 1/320

Page 125

BLIND SPOT
Negaprion brevirostris

A startled shark reacts defensively to Hanli's sudden arrival in its blind spot. This was not the most rigorously planned approach… Despite years of experience, Hanli is not immune from making this sort of mistake. Generally speaking, you must assume that the animal has noticed you approaching and as far as possible let it come and go as it pleases. That's the challenge for freedivers with limited diving time.

Bahamas, Tiger Beach • December 2013
📷 29 mm • f 13 • 1/200

Page 126

PLAYMATES
Galeocerdo cuvier

This image is extremely valuable to me as it is the only one where Leina and Hanli appear together. We ran short of time during this stay in the Bahamas and I'd been sick for the second time in two months, probably thanks to intense travelling and lack of sleep. Leina and Hanli were extremely patient with me. The photo shows them both swimming with a tiger shark which doesn't seem in the least disturbed.

Bahamas, Tiger Beach • December 2013 📷 24 mm • f 9 • 1/320

Pages 128 & 129

CATCH ME IF YOU CAN…
Galeocerdo cuvier

I can't resist a bit of fun, just like Leina. The tiger shark is already far away when she reaches its depth. But she's not trying to get any closer. Leina's posture suggests that she wants to remove the line that is hooked at the side of the shark's mouth. Countless sharks in the area still have hooks in their flesh or bear scars around the mouth.

Bahamas, Tiger Beach • December 2013 📷 24 mm • f 6.3 • 1/160

Page 130

EMMA AND LEINA
Galeocerdo cuvier

Although Leina's position is not strictly correct, I can hardly hold it against her, since this is only her third dive with a tiger shark. Not just any tiger shark: Emma is a wonderful playmate who never shows any sign of shyness. This image allows you to appreciate the size difference, although the 35 mm camera lens slightly distorts the perspective.

Bahamas, Tiger Beach • December 2013 📷 35 mm • f 8 • 1/200

Pages 132 & 133

South Africa, Gansbaai • July 2010 📷 20 mm • f 9 • 1/320

GREAT WHITE SHARK CHARGING
Carcharodon carcharias

Your first encounter with a great white shark is etched in your mind forever. This is especially true when, irritated to see his bait get away, it launches into an intimidation charge, swerving at the last second.

This image was shot in the winter in Gansbaai, South Africa. I was safely immersed in a cage. There's a first time for everything.

Page 135

FACIAL SIGNS
Carcharodon carcharias

This picture says a lot about the life led by the adult female. Like all of her kind she bears the marks of her incessant struggles with humans or prey. The remora waits patiently for the next opportunity to feed. People don't always realize how rarely sharks eat. They can go for several months without eating thanks to the size of their liver where they store squalene, a lipid with a high calorific value.

Mexico, Isla de Guadalupe • October 2013
📷 60 mm • f 7.1 • 1/200

Page 136

THE CAGE AS A SYMBOL
Carcharodon carcharias

The first question I am asked when I explain that I photograph sharks is invariably: 'in a cage?' This question speaks volumes about sharks' perennial reputation as dangerous creatures. The cage was omnipresent when diving with great whites and we took refuge in it whenever an individual proved too territorial. However, these are exceptional cases and very often sharks' behaviour is linked to the presence of food, which is completely understandable. With all other species – without exception – dives take place without a cage and with no protection other than the greatest responsiveness to sharks' body language. If I have to put a little distance between myself and a shark, I hold out my camera casing, since contact with a hard object is enough to discourage a shark from investigating any further.

Mexico, Isla de Guadalupe • September 2012 📷 38 mm • f 11 • 1/500

Page 138

INTIMIDATION
Carcharodon carcharias

We had barely entered the water when this 4-metre-long female arrived. Attracted by a fresh tuna head hanging from the cage, she showed a younger accompanying male that she was the stronger of the two. Once he swam away, she chose the diver who was most nervous that day and launched an intimidation attack. The diver used his shark-billy to keep her away. All three divers took shelter. I knelt on the cage, alone.

Mexico, Isla de Guadalupe • October 2013
📷 34 mm • f 6.3 • 1/160

Page 139

FULL FRONTAL ATTACK
Carcharodon carcharias

Having forced three divers to retreat to the safety of the cage, the territorial female comes to get her due. This is what I imagine until the moment when, opening her jaws to take the tuna head, she sees me and decides to intimidate me instead. Her gaze fixes on me and in a split second, she closes the two-metre gap between us and tries to bite me. I push the camera casing at her with all my might and she bites the dome's protective rubber cap. I'm stuck between her and the cage's superstructure; I have no room for manoeuvre. I must wait for the distracting stream of bubbles from my fellow divers who are back in the cage to free me from her pressure. As she rolls to move aside, I want to photograph her but to my horror, I realize that water has leaked into the casing. One of the divers cuts the rope holding the tuna head and the shark dives for it. I go back up, holding the dome downwards to avoid further contact between water and my camera. More shaken than injured, I get out of the water, unharmed. The attack was so determined that this is the first time I felt really threatened.

Mexico, Isla de Guadalupe • October 2012
📷 24 mm • f 6.3 • 1/160

Page 137

SYMBOLIC OF THE BAIT
Carcharodon carcharias

Make no mistake; even though we are in the 'Mecca' of great whites, the probability that they will spontaneously come to see us is close to zero. We often have to bait sharks for hours on end before seeing them. This year, some groups of divers only enjoyed one sighting out of the five foreseen. A thawed tuna is hardly motivating when sharks enjoy abundant live food in the Guadelupe waters. However, these hugely opportunistic animals always end up approaching it!

Mexico, Isla de Guadalupe • October 2013 📷 24 mm • f 5.6 • 1/125

THE TROUBLEMAKER
Carcharodon carcharias

No need to make excuses for the criminal appearance of this young male. As soon as we entered the water, all three of us knew that we had to keep an eye on this highly territorial specimen. After ten minutes, he came closer and started attacking me. Using my camera casing, I pushed him away three times. Martin's turn comes next, then finally the third diver. We decided to abort the dive. This shark was too insistent and other sharks present were already starting to approach.

Bahamas, Tiger Beach • September 2012 📷 24 mm • f 9 • 1/320

Page 142

MARTIN AND THE GREAT WHITE SHARK
Carcharodon carcharias

Martin has spent the last ten years flirting with sharks in every ocean around the globe. There aren't many people alive who can 'handle' a fact-finding visit from an adult great white shark. This female is 5 metres long and weighs approximately 1.5 tons. Thankfully (in Martin's own words), she's a 'player', who greets him without any aggressiveness, seemingly enjoying the contact. After Martin took a mere five minutes to earn her trust, we spent over an hour in her company. An exceptional and highly emotional meeting between two extraordinary beings.

Mexico, Isla de Guadalupe • September 2012 📷 24 mm • f 7.1 • 1/200

Page 144

TRAILING EDGE
Carcharodon carcharias

Almost every adult shark has fins with damaged trailing edges. To take this photograph, I let this great white shark climb up towards me before pivoting vertically at the moment of contact to find myself above him and facing in his direction.

Mexico, Isla de Guadalupe • October 2013
📷 27 mm • f 5.6 • 1/125

Page 145

AN AWKWARD REPUTATION
Carcharodon carcharias

One species of shark especially suffers from prejudice based on appearance: the great white. How can one photograph it without emphasizing this negative image? It took me a lot of time and a great deal of imagination to find an interesting angle that presented its true colours, without showing the face that earns the fish its reputation as a man-eater.

Mexico, Isla de Guadalupe • September 2012
📷 24 mm • f 5.6 • 1/125

Page 143

INTIMACY
Carcharodon carcharias

At first sight, the relative size and proximity seem so improbable that you think it must have been edited. This photograph captures an exceptional encounter between a 5-metre female weighing approximately 1.5 tons and Martin, a shark-loving diver friend. We shared this great white shark's territory for a little more than an hour. She did not show any sign of aggressiveness during that time, sometimes even following us to the surface to be stroked. This is without doubt one of the most beautiful encounters of this journey of initiation.

Mexico, Isla de Guadalupe • September 2012 📷 27 mm • f 7.1 • 1/200

Page 147

MOTHERHOOD
Carcharodon carcharias

This beautiful female will give birth at any moment: her round shape gives the game away easily. This image allows us to appreciate the characteristic shape of the great white shark, with its large body right up to the beginning of the tail.

Mexico, Isla de Guadalupe • September 2012
📷 24 mm • f 5.6 • 1/125

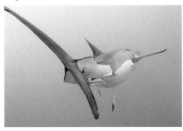

CONTACT WITH
A GREAT WHITE SHARK
Carcharodon carcharias

The most astonishing encounter… I was trying to document the body section at the base of the tail of the great white shark. My first attempts had proved inconclusive.

In order to position myself above the shark in front of its tail, I let him come up through the water to me and I swim towards him, convinced that he will avoid me at the last minute, thus allowing me to photograph this part of him. This beautiful male decided otherwise and did not flinch from his trajectory. We bumped against one other. I managed to let my body slide along his, but without managing to avoid contact with his tail.

These feats produced these two shots. In the second, you can see that the shark is still in shock, as he only just manages to avoid his companion.

Mexico, Isla de Guadalupe • October 2013
35 mm • f 6.3 • 1/160
24 mm • f 6.3 • 1/160

AFTER THE FEAST
Carcharodon carcharias

This image is doubly meaningful. Whilst the various scars tell many tales of past combats, giving an insight in the difficult lives of sharks, this trailing intestine is the only remaining sign of the predator's last nocturnal hunt.

This probably explains this great white shark's placid, well-fed behaviour as he accompanies us for more than an hour, seemingly enjoying our presence as much as we enjoy his.

Mexico, Isla de Guadalupe • September 2012   24 mm • f 7.1 • 1/200

SEA LIONS AT PLAY
Carcharodon carcharias

Although sea lions are firmly on the sharks' menu, they fearlessly let sharks come close and are perfectly aware of the safety distance they must keep when visibility is good. The first image shows a sea lion diving from the surface where it was playing, as if to mock its main predator. In the second image, the sea lion seems to be coming down to greet the shark. The sea lion's agility and quick reactions protect it from shark attacks. Sea lions have been seen biting sharks to chase them away from their underwater playground. However, once visibility decreases, the situation drastically changes and extreme vigilance is needed once again. The same applies to professional divers wanting to work outside a cage. In South Africa, at least 6 metres' visibility is required within the framework of the licence authorizing this type of activity.

Mexico, Isla de Guadalupe • October 2013   24 mm • f 5.6 • 1/125

GLIDING UNDERWATER
Carcharodon carcharias

This is one of the few images taken from the cage. I was coming back up from my first dive and had watched sea lions near the boat. I was secretly hoping that they would tease this female, but to no avail. I spent an hour watching her turning back and forth under the surface to capture the moment when she glides through the water in a perfect straight line, just like a plane.

Mexico, Isla de Guadalupe • October 2013   70 mm • f 6.3 • 1/125

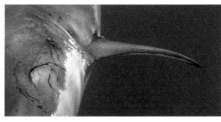

PRENUPTIALS
Carcharodon carcharias

The cause of these bite marks is not in doubt: this 4-metre adult female has reached breeding age. To withstand prenuptial bites like this, the skin of female sharks is thicker than that of their male counterparts, and wounds heal in just a few weeks before disappearing completely.

Mexico, Isla de Guadalupe • October 2013
24 mm • f 5.6 • 1/125

Pages 156 & 157

RELENTLESS ATTACKS

I never tire of this spectacle. Cape gannets (Morus capensis) take huge pleasure in this merciless hunt. Dive-bombing the sardines near the surface of the water, their attacks clash with those of dolphins, sharks and the occasional whale. The birds dive to a depth of up to 10 metres, sometimes having to catch their prey by swimming after them. From time to time, we find a dead young bird with a broken neck, having miscalculated its entry angle. We get into the water in these intimidating conditions. Close to the surface, we are startled by the noise of the birds hitting the water all around us at more than 120 kilometres an hour.

South Africa, Port Saint Johns • July 2011 • 70 mm • f 22 • 1/100

Page 159

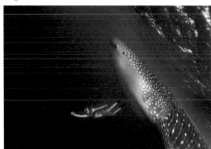

LEINA AND THE WHALE SHARK
Rhincodon typus

Despite some sporadic encounters with whale sharks in Hawaii, Leina had never enjoyed an opportunity to observe them. In Djibouti, she spent several hours every day alongside them, following the rhythm of their feeding and enjoying truly intimate moments with them. On several occasions, the shark diverted from its path to come to meet her. She is shown diving a few metres from a shark that seems totally undisturbed by her presence.

Djibouti, Gulf of Tadjoura • January 2014 • 14 mm • f 5 • 1/100

Page 161

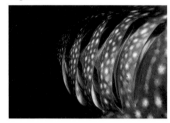

PUZZLING PERFECTION
Rhincodon typus

Jules Verne and Leonardo da Vinci immediately spring to mind when I look at this example of mechanic perfection. I can only wonder what the imagination of these great minds might have come up with, had they been able to observe these whale sharks' gills.

Djibouti, Gulf of Tadjoura • January 2014 • 24 mm • f 5.6 • 1/125

Page 162

WHALE SHARK AT NIGHT
Rhincodon typus

At the bottom of the Gulf of Tadjoura in Djibouti, young whale sharks gather from September to January and feast to their heart's content. The plankton accumulates, moved by eastern winds, allowing several hundred sharks to find the food necessary for their development. This young male of approximately 5 metres kept us company for more than three hours in the dark of night, feeding from a plankton column formed from the deep sea to the water surface, right under the light projector set up close to the ship. Most of the time, he tilts his body vertically to suck the micro-organisms. This image was taken on his first pass. Thanks to the additional lighting of my videographer friend René Heuzey, I captured this exceptional image as the shark was caught between the two light sources.

Djibouti, Gulf of Tadjoura • January 2014 • 24 mm • f 7.1 • 1/200

Page 165

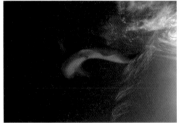

PLANKTON COLUMN
Rhincodon typus

This photograph would be difficult to understand without a caption. The upward 'plait' is actually plankton rising from the depths of the ocean to form a cloud under the light of the projector at the surface. The silhouette is that of a whale shark who has come to check that this good luck is really happening. After several passes, the shark will tilt vertically to 'pump' the content of the column for three whole hours.

Djibouti, Gulf of Tadjoura • January 2014 • 14 mm • f 2.8 • 1/4

Page 166

THE WHALE SHARK'S FUNNEL MOUTH
Rhincodon typus

You can only admire the perfect structure of the body of the whale shark, which can almost completely open its jaws to form a huge funnel enabling it to filter a volume of water in twenty-four hours equivalent to the contents of an Olympic size swimming pool.

Djibouti, Gulf of Tadjoura • January 2014 • 15 mm • f 5.1 • 1/100

Page 168

SOURCE OF LIFE

Plankton represent the basic staple for countless species. Before my nocturnal dives to encounter whale sharks, I had never given much consideration to this life form. This image allows one to make out clearly the seething mass of these microorganisms attracted to the surface by the light of the projector. They form a column reaching far down into the depths, gathering in a cloud near the surface. More concentrated in the shaft of light, the plankton whirl in every direction but never collide. I could have watched this endless dance all night if it hadn't been for all the crabs nipping me, eager to join in the feast.

Djibouti, Gulf of Tadjoura • January 2014   📷 14 mm • f 13 • 1/6

Pages 169 & 171

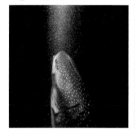

IN THE LIMELIGHT
Rhincodon typus

The trusting whale shark has positioned itself under the projector to suck the continuous flow of plankton, its body distorting as it absorbs the food. Tilted vertically, it sucks the entire plankton column before departing, sated, three hours later. Of all the situations I experienced throughout these four years of adventure, this one touched me the most through the almost divine character of an animal feeding on a shaft of light.

Djibouti, Gulf of Tadjoura • January 2014
📷 24 mm • f 5 • 1/100   📷 14 mm • f 4 • 1/60

Pages 172 & 173

FLIGHT OF THE CORMORANTS

We were on our way back from observing great white shark attacks on young seals on Seal Island when we came across thousands of cormorants returning to the coast. The ocean was like a mirror, only their wing beats disturbing the surface. They took to the air as the boat opened a passage into this surreal universe.

South Africa, False Bay • July 2010   📷 70 mm • f 22 • 1/125

Page 192

INTIMIDATION
Carcharhinus limbatus

Black tips aren't shy and will approach you easily, particularly if there's food around. Most individuals are not disturbed by the presence of a diver. But sometimes they don't like it, and this one lets me know that I should back off... which I do.

South Africa, Aliwal Shoal • July 2011   📷 24 mm • f 11 • 1/500

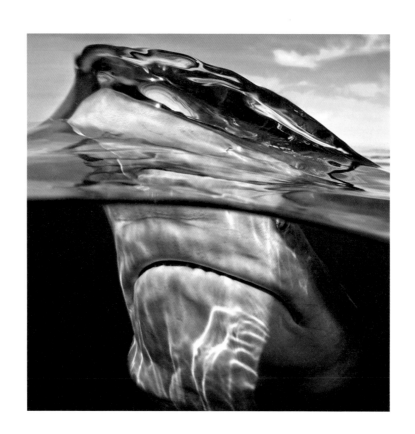